Victoria

The Art of Taking Tea

Victoria

The Art of Taking Tea

Kim Waller

Hearst Books

A Division of Sterling Publishing Co., Inc.

New York

This book was previously published as a hardcover.

Designer: Amy Henderson
Produced by Smallwood & Stewart, Inc.
New York City

The Library of Congress has cataloged the hardcover
edition as follows:
The art of taking tea / the editors of Victoria magazine.
          p.cm.
ISBN 1-58816-005-X
1. Cookery (Tea) 2. Tea. I. Victoria (New York, N.Y.)
TX817.T3 A78 2001
641.3'372—dc21

                                        00-063210

10 9 8 7 6 5 4 3 2 1

First Paperback Edition 2005
Published by Hearst Books
A Division of Sterling Publishing Co., Inc.
387 Park Avenue South, New York, NY 10016

Hearst Books is proud to continue the superb
style, quality, and tradition of *Victoria* magazine with
every book we publish. On our beautifully illustrated
pages you will always find inspiration and ideas about
the subjects you love.

Victoria is a trademark owned by Hearst Magazines
Property, Inc., in USA, and Hearst Communications,
Inc., in Canada. Hearst Books is a trademark owned by
Hearst Communications, Inc.

For information about custom editions, special sales,
premium and corporate purchases, please contact
Sterling Special Sales Department at 800-805-5489 or
specialsales@sterlingpub.com.

Distributed in Canada by Sterling Publishing
c/o Canadian Manda Group, 165 Dufferin Street
Toronto, Ontario, Canada M6K 3H6

Distributed in Australia by Capricorn Link
(Australia) Pty. Ltd.
P.O. Box 704, Windsor, NSW 2756 Australia

Manufactured in China

ISBN 1-58816-494-2

Foreword

Wherever I travel, my hosts almost always ask first if I would like a cup of tea. Somehow, this universal gesture of hospitality sets all to rights, even among strangers. In Japan, I sat shoeless and cross-legged on the floor of a family's home to sip green tea from small cups. In Russia, an elderly woman prepared a delicious herbal tea for me, promising, "Drink this, and you will be as strong as a bear, as swift as a deer, as wise as an owl." How I wished I had that recipe to take home!

To me, though, tea does have extraordinary powers: I've proved it. One wintry day when my son, Gene, was about ten, I braved his room, full of rough-housing friends and flying footballs, to invite the boys to a proper tea. Pouring Earl Grey through a silver strainer into my pink lusterware cups, I asked if they preferred lemon or milk. "Milk, please," they said in unison. For the ten minutes it took to down the tea and a plate of fresh-baked cookies, they were totally civilized—as impressed by this gentle ceremony as I was by their manners.

Tea and *Victoria* have been close friends for many years. We hope you enjoy our newest tribute to the civilizing cup.

Peggy Kennedy

VICTORIA

The Cherished Leaf

Could there be anything more elemental than a cup of tea? Yet in its clear depths lies a great saga of East and West, of ceremony and enterprise.

Its liquor is like the sweetest dew of heaven," wrote Lu Yu, tea's first scholar-poet, circa A.D. 750. Even then tea was valued in China, its land of origin, for those medicinal qualities we are only now able to document. But tea does more than brace the body, said Lu Yu; it opens the eye of the spirit, it suffuses one with peace.

Tea has its myths, and so do tea cups: On Wedgwood jasperware, goddesses frolic.

After his influential book, *Ch'a Ching*, or "Classic of Tea," nine hundred years would pass before European sea traders imported tea to Holland, and from there to England. Suddenly, the exotic elixir of China was all the rage among stylish folk.

Tea has always offered a lovely excuse for collecting accoutrements, such as these lustrous vintage cups.

In seventeenth-century Holland, guests at grand tea parties drank as many as fifty small cups with rich cakes, followed by brandy and raisins. At the English court, King Charles II's queen, the Portuguese Catherine de Braganza, popularized tea. The fashion filtered from coffeehouse to manor house, "cheering the whole land from the palace to the cottage," as one observer put it. Initially, tea was so precious that it was locked away in strongboxes. Demand for this and other profitable luxuries of the East, including silk and porcelain, launched the powerful British East India Company on the high seas to Canton. Indeed, the China trade eventually started England on a tea-drinking way of life, forever replacing ale as the national breakfast drink. By the 1750s, Samuel Johnson, for one, had become such a "hardened and shameless tea-drinker" that he swore his kettle barely ever cooled.

Enamored of "the infusion of this fascinating plant," Samuel Johnson boasted of being a person "who with tea amuses the evening, with tea solaces the midnight, and with tea welcomes the morning."

An open display of china meant for everyday use beckons each morning in a Danish country kitchen.

A WORLD OF CUSTOMS

Perhaps we'd be surprised to see well-dressed guests slurping tea from their saucers, but that was once the custom in England and America. Certainly, the habit cooled the steaming beverage a bit.

Long before the West made a social event of tea, however, Zen Buddhist monks brought the leaf from China to Japan, where in 1588 the tea master Rikyu formalized a poetic ritual still practiced today, a ceremony requiring a space adorned only with a picture, a simple flower arrangement, and the beauty of the tea utensils. In the relationship of host to guests, of each object to another, students of the Japanese tea ceremony find a calm beyond the ruckus of the everyday world.

Strong or weak? In the still~maintained Victorian custom, it is the role of the hostess to prepare each guest's teacup: a leisurely, considerate propriety.

THE CHINA
TO HAVE

If you are sailing from China to England with silk and tea on board, the last thing you want to do is get the cargo wet. Water ruins both products, so they were carried in the middle of the ship. Fortunately, the perfect ballast to stack in the hold in the 1700s was exactly what all of Europe and the American colonies were clamor-

A contemporary teapot from China speaks of centuries-old design.

ing for: Chinese porcelain. Although many Western attempts were made to approximate its fine hardness (based on a clay called kaolin that withstood high-temperature firing), none really succeeded. People bought porcelain off the ships or placed orders with the Chinese potters of Jindezhen to create a full set,

Porcelain, in this case of new manufacture, ensures purity of taste for even the subtlest teas.

It is the most popular china pattern ever known, made in many hundreds of versions for hundreds of years. It teases our imagination: Those figures hurrying across the bridge, the doves, the boat seem like characters in search of an author.

of a well-born maiden, Koong Shee, in love with Chang, a lowly secretary. Forbidding her to marry beneath her station, her father, a wealthy mandarin, locks her up until her arranged wedding to another. But the lovers escape with the help of a gardener, racing over a bridge

The Mystery and Legend of Blue Willow China

This much-loved china pattern has appeared in many colors, but blue-and-white has always been the favorite. On this modern teapot you can see the little boat, perhaps intended as the safe passage to happiness for the doomed lovers of legend.

And yes, there is a legend. But it was devised well after the pattern became popular. At first, English potters copied Chinese design elements⁓here a pagoda, there a bridge⁓on their affordable earthenware. Sometime in the late 1700s the willow pattern we know was born in the factories of Stoke on Trent, and was immediately a hit.

The best-known tale inspired by the pattern first appeared in an English magazine in 1849. It tells

to hide on the island. There they are found by the furious father. As his murderous wrath descends upon the lovers, the merciful gods transform them into doves, eternally paired in flight. "I wouldn't be one to deny it," wrote an anonymous poet, "For the little blue dove and her mate / Forever are flying together / Across my Willowware plate."

perhaps adorned with the family crest, and well worth waiting for.

Such was the rage for "china" in England that it was soon being displayed "on every chimney-piece, to the tops of ceilings, until it became a grievance," carped Daniel Defoe. (Proudly displayed china is still a stalwart of English decorating.) Though fools for beautiful china, those early collectors were hardly foolish: Glorious handpainted Chinese export wares are highly valued today by museums. (One of the very best collections can be seen at the Peabody Museum in Salem, Massachusetts.) While England and Europe searched madly for a source of kaolin, their potters swiftly turned out inexpensive copies of the prized import in earthenware and stoneware. Kaolin was finally discovered in Germany. To this day, no substance is kinder to tea than hard-paste porcelain, which imparts no flavor of its own.

Into tiny pots filled with loose leaves, the Chinese pour water again and again for small tastings of tea.

A TEA SOMMELIER

As James Labe approaches diners, carrying his tray of select tea leaves, few realize they are about to be inducted into a mystery. This is a man with a mission, as expert in his field as a master wine steward. At a New York restaurant where he consults, James and the restaurant's chef have transformed the experience of afternoon tea into a tea-tasting adventure. For a piquant pear salad with blue cheese, first-flush Darjeeling is the match. Tung ting oolong stands up to hearty pan-roasted bison with cherry sauce. A chocolate dessert begs for a slightly flowery bai hao oolong.

A tea importer as well, James introduces customers to the best teas of a certain year. As he unfolds the story of each choice, from pale Silver Needle white to pellet-shaped Jasmine Pearl, people who have never before studied tea leaves can see and smell the difference. The culinary explorers taste, then say, "Yes! I see what you mean." James smiles. Mission accomplished.

With food, teas are as deliciously subtle as wines.

A MIRACULOUS PLANT

Many of us rely on the convenience of a tea bag. We dunk it a few times, then discard it. Perked with lemon or milk, perhaps a bit of sugar, our cuppa, as the British say, is just fine. Familiar. Handy. Hot.

Imagine, now, a terraced hillside, green and misty, in India or Taiwan. Between curving rows of chest-high tea plants, shawled women move slowly, pinching off only the youngest leaves, perhaps some with tender buds.

If the tea plant, *Camellia sinensis*, were left alone, it would grow into a wild, sturdy tree thirty-five feet tall. But in the long-cultivated tea gardens of the East, it is tended as carefully as the grapevines of Champagne — and harvested far more frequently.

This one miraculous plant (with many sub-varieties) gives us an amazing range of subtle brews. Soil, climate, and elevation, regular or unexpected

"With each sip I taste / The fire that gives its heat, / The water that gives its wetness, / The leaf that gives its spell."

—The Minister of Leaves

Creamware and gleaming silver—a happy English marriage that has lasted since the eighteenth century.

There is something about the very essence of tea that suggests a bit of ceremony in the serving. For eighteenth-century aristocrats, as for proper Victorians, a full silver tea service on its tray, or salver, flashed a beautiful message of hospitality⁓with entirely intentional overtones of status and

Putting a Formal Shine on Teatime

You needn't aspire to own a complete silver tea set. Instead, collect shapely and often fanciful accoutrements that add luster to your table. Aside from the usual teapot, hot water urn, and coffeepot, here are some other pieces to collect.

Creamer and Sugar This most useful duo will always shine at dinner parties and family gatherings.

Strainer Place over the cup to catch loose tea leaves as you pour from the pot. Or use it to strain the seeds from squeezed lemons.

Sugar Tongs and Lemon Forks They're showy yet delicate. Use them as helpers on an hors d'oeuvres tray.

Tea Caddies Of course, these would be lovely on the vanity. Better yet, preserve your prize first-flush Darjeeling in style.

Teaspoons Hunt for your engraved first or last initial in antiques shops.

prosperity. Silversmiths lavished their artistry on every element of the tea equipage, and for generations the silver tea set was among the proudest of heirlooms. But after World War II, all that polishing and propriety seemed just too much bother. The result is that fine silver tea implements became widely available for collectors with a gleam in their eye. They remain so today.

weather conditions—all affect flavor. But most important, the method of curing the leaves determines which of three basic styles of tea you will drink: green, oolong, or black.

Once picked, all tea leaves are dried enough to eliminate moisture and start the process of oxidizing, a chemical change known—misleadingly—as fermentation. For delicate green tea (the favorite in China), that process is very quickly arrested by firing, or heating. Heartier black tea (the favorite in the West) is fermented much longer. Oolong falls between, in both processing and flavor. Rolling and bruising the leaves to release the juices is important, too, and may be done several times between repeated firings until the leaves are finally crisp and dry. Traditionally, all this was accomplished by hand (and sometimes by foot); today, in major tea gardens, machines and ovens have taken over the jobs.

Match teacups and saucers in form or spirit, if not in pattern. Collecting odd ones is more fun if you look for one color or a particular maker.

Fill a newly purchased gem with a small bouquet and enjoy the sweet view.

"Each cup of tea represents an imaginary voyage."

—Catherine Douzel

Thus did hostesses once inquire about one's preference, meaning, basically: green or black?

China tea, including the long-popular scented jasmine, has the reputation of being a meditative sip, while India tea is considered bracing. But so considerable are the differences among the teas of India alone, the world's largest producer, that saying "India" to a tea connoisseur is like saying "blue" to Rembrandt. And what of Japan, Formosa, Taiwan, Sri Lanka? They, too, produce lovely teas worth knowing. As for the supermarket tea bag, its contents probably come from Australia, where the leaves are harvested by machine.

New, vintage, or antique, a rose-patterned tea set lends any gathering the mood of a garden party.

Tea set:
6 cups,
saucers and
plates.   £55.

Bathroom
cabinet
£62.00

Getting out and about to pay afternoon calls on one's friends and social connections was a pleasant duty for Victorians of leisure. Hostesses, on their "at-home day," were sure to proffer meringues or bread-and-butter sandwiches as thin as their teacups; guests supplied

At Home to Friends ∼ No Calling Card Required

polite chatter and, just possibly, a scintillating bit of gossip.

Now that calling cards have evolved into business cards and friends connect through e-mail, we tend to look back on those stuffy parlor formalities with amusement. And maybe some envy? Imagine having time just to sip and visit and nibble, to catch up on the doings of sons and daughters. So why not borrow the best of an old custom and announce your own "at-home" afternoon, perhaps on a winter weekend? It needn't be a grand affair. Simply get out pretty teacups and those little linen napkins you rarely use. Then brew the tea and light the fire: Friends are coming to call.

No wonder Victorian teatimes were gracious: The butler did it. To make hostessing without help easier, you can brew some extra-strong tea ahead of time. When ready to serve, dilute it in the cup (or teapot) with just-boiled water. Don't worry; it will be hot enough.

Meet a Friend
for Tea

SOME FAVORITE VENUES

At country inns and city salons, teatime is once again a stylish event. And the range of teas, tastes, and settings you will discover are far from ordinary.

When you think of visiting a tea parlor, do you imagine nibbling buttery crumpets at a little chintz-covered table? Today's spots for tea offer so many other experiences. In recent decades, countless American tearooms of distinctive style have blossomed across the country, from Pasadena to Portland. Whether their approach is serenely Asian, sublimely English, or inventively New Age, the best venues always include that most gratifying of tea's accompaniments — a sense of peace and renewal.

BOSTON TEA PARTY

If you assume that college students can't survive without coffee, step into Tealuxe, a modern little tea bar located at the heart of Harvard Square in Cambridge, Massachusetts. Yes, there is indeed one

An American tea bar: sleek yet warm, with a hint of Paris.

coffee on the menu for unwavering devotees. The rest of the menu, however, offers more than a hundred different teas, including many herbal and floral tisanes, that hail from fourteen countries. At any hour from dawn until midnight, you're likely to see students, professors, tourists, and Boston matrons sipping their favorite Earl Grey (there are six on the menu) or eagerly trying the newest brewed-to-order organic green gunpowder or ginger-ginseng herbal. Dark navy-blue walls, dark wood, and a gleaming copper bar suggest the atmosphere of an old Parisian coffee bar, which is pretty much the image Katharine Bowen Walsh had in mind when she designed Tealuxe. Says her husband and co-owner, Bruce Fernie, "We wanted men to feel as comfortable here as women. And they do: One even wrote his novel here. It's a great place for a low-cost, alcohol-free date, and women feel fine coming in alone."

"Tea, though ridiculed by those who are naturally coarse in their nervous systems… will always be the favored beverage of the intellectual."

—Thomas DeQuincy

Meeting friends? Order the big "party pot" or, better yet, small pots of different teas—then share and compare.

As the waitress pours your freshly brewed pot of tea, the conversation over the table stops for a moment, and all eyes are fixed on the amber liquid filling the cups—it is one of those slow-motion ceremonies of expectation, like watching Champagne rise in a crystal flute. How did the tea you are about to raise to your lips arrive here at this exact time and place? What were the stages of its journey from a hillside in India or a tea garden in China or Sri Lanka?

Let's say that you've ordered a Darjeeling from India. There may be a hundred growers in that region, whose products can be as different as one Côtes du Rhône wine from another. Moreover, each of their pickings will vary somewhat, depending on weather conditions. As soon as the tea is cured, samples are dispatched to special customers around the world. They must swiftly taste and decide whether to place an order, since the rest of the harvest will shortly go to auction in Calcutta.

Here the representatives of major tea brokers bid and buy Darjeeling in large lots. (Assam, India's black tea, is auctioned in

another nearby city.) "Brokers in Hamburg, Germany, have traditionally been the suppliers of all teas for most of Europe, and three main brokers on our West Coast supply America," says Sebastian Beckwith of In Pursuit of Tea, a boutique importer of high-grade un-blended teas. Today, tea is still shipped to retailers in sturdy wooden chests ("made of plywood these days"), either by regular mail or air express.

Sebastian and his partners travel throughout Southeast Asia in search of distinctive teas produced by small, traditional gardens, where mass-production methods have not yet intruded. "We're interested in the differences in lots," he says, "not the con-sistency that large importers require." In the process, he has sat cross-legged before small cups from India to Taiwan and made many international friends. Recently, impelled to go even farther back

Most of the teas we are accustomed to drinking are blends created for consistent flavor. But many connoisseurs prefer "true" teas, the better to savor their unique qualities.

in time, he journeyed by truck and river-boat to nearly impenetrable country in northern Laos. Here, close to China's Yunan province, where tea began, he met with villagers who still smoke a rough, strong tea for their own use over an open fire. "It was," he says, "like returning to the dawn of tea culture."

As in Russia, tea is sipped in clear glass mugs, the better to appreciate the different hues. Only a few cakes and pastries are served, but the tea menu itself makes for delicious reading. Extra Fancy Bai Hao Taiwan Oolong, for example, is described as "toward the darker side of oolongs, with a caramel scent; flavors peachy, nutty, woody." And you can take Tealuxe's offerings home, all complete with brewing instructions.

Served in clear glass cups, tea has a chance to show off its true colors.

"We've hit a nerve," says Bruce. "People who thought tea was something you drank when you were sick or visited your grandma are realizing, Wow! Look at all these flavors and colors! Others are very seriously into the health and medicinal qualities."

This refreshing herbal iced tea is flavored with fruit and rose hips.

Traditional temptations: Forget dinner.

TEATIME RULES BRITANNIA

Disregard the maps: The British Isles float on a sea of tea. From Edinburgh to Bath, the instinctive reaction to any event—tears, triumph, or rain—is to put on the kettle.

A proper afternoon tea, however, that near-meal of petite sweets and crustless sandwiches, is an occasion in itself. (It is not to be confused with high tea, a simple supper featuring cold meats.) Fortunately, you needn't go to Devon for clotted cream to slather on your scones or to Scotland for buttery shortbread. Hotels and tearooms from New York to Melbourne honor the indulgent custom, whose purpose is to blend sociability with satiety.

"The cup of tea on arrival at a country house is a thing which... I particularly enjoy." —P. G. Wodehouse

A three-tiered tray for goodies saves space on an intimate tea table.

THE ENGLISH SUBLIME

If you don't happen to own an English country house but dream of brisk walks to the sea, croquet on the lawn, and a sumptuous afternoon tea, you can step straight into the dream at Chewton Glen.

Consistently rated the top country-house hotel in England, this haven on seventy acres of England's south coast excels at making guests feel at home in the purest English style ~ a relaxed elegance. Amid the antiques and fresh flowers, no note is off-key, no whispered wish goes untended, whether it's for a tennis racket if you left yours at home or a bottle of Champagne in your room at midnight.

"The ideal setting for tea on a cold day is a nice deep armchair by our fireside," says Peter Crome, the hotel's general manager. In warm weather, the terrace fronting a sweep of lawns is preferred. Of course, staying in a house that dates from the eighteenth century certainly excites the senses, including one's taste for tea.

Here you can choose from two classic versions of afternoon tea. For those who can't quite face three tiers of delicacies but don't mind sticky fingers, there's the Devon Cream Tea, featuring warm scones, clotted cream, jam, and a selection of fruit. Full Afternoon Tea includes the works: scones and jam, a selection of fruit and cream pastries, and sandwiches.

"One can certainly get creative with teatime foods," says Peter, "but at Chewton Glen people expect the traditional." That usually means sandwiches of smoked salmon, cream cheese and cucumber, and egg salad with watercress—all served on a silver tray table. No need to rush through this lovely ceremony. There is plenty of time for another cup, whether you prefer leaf-brewed jasmine, gunpowder, Lapsang souchong or English breakfast tea. Afterward, a leisurely stroll is certainly in order. It's only a ten-minute walk to the cliffs over the Solent, the channel that divides England from the Isle of Wight.

"In nothing is the English genius for domesticity more notably declared than in the institution of afternoon tea."

—George Gissing

JAPANESE STYLE IN NEW YORK CITY

A uniformed doorman is always there to welcome you at Takashimaya's store on Manhattan's Fifth Avenue. It's a sleek emporium of sophisticated contemporary design where every vase, pillow, and plate has an almost sculptural purity. Even the exquisite floral arrangements speak of the less that is more. Some who bustle in are not there to shop, however. They've come with a friend for lunch or afternoon tea at the Tea Box, one flight down from street level, a retreat where East joins West in flavor and decor. Order the bento box luncheon, served in a lacquered tray of four compartments, and you'll be served an intriguing balance of small dishes: perhaps a delicate fish salad, thin-sliced steak with soba noodles, watercress topped with a fried oyster, and tea-flavored rice. "I change the offerings every day," says chef

Served in a lacquered bento box, a meal of small, tasty dishes becomes a display of individual gifts.

ASIAN AESTHETICS

You needn't study with a master of the tea ceremony or sit cross-legged on the floor to entertain your friends amid calm and simplicity. In fact, the keynotes of the Asian aesthetic—natural materials such as straw and bamboo, an emphasis on form rather than pattern—are remarkably in tune with contemporary taste. To replicate the mood of an Asian tea salon at home, consider using a plain porcelain or metal teapot. Another choice: the highly collectible little Yi-xing Chinese teapots, made in various shapes since the Ming Dynasty of a special clay. (Since the clay absorbs and ultimately enriches tea flavors, these are usually dedicated to one type of tea only.) A handcarved wooden scoop for the tea leaves, small ceramic cups with-

"Tea...became more than an idealization of the form of drinking: it is a religion of the art of life."

—Kakuzo Okakura

out handles, a handwoven cloth or split-bamboo mats, even cookies flavored with lotus or ginger or burdock—these can often be purchased at Asian emporiums. Equally important are the flowers. Instead of making an opulent bouquet, try your hand at a spare, Japanese-style arrangement, in which the balance and contrast of individual stems and blossoms focus the spirit as well as the eye.

Christine Mullen, "depending on the season, and because so many people come here frequently."

Along with light dishes, the menu offers an astonishing thirty different teas to choose from, including herbal. If you're baffled, the waiter will suggest one to suit either your lunch or the menu of sweets and savories that is served after three o'clock. (Even the sweets can surprise: black rice pudding, sublime green tea mousse.) Perfectly brewed, your tea arrives in a ceramic pot to pour into silvery-gray teacups, with a lollipop-like rock sugar stirrer for those who like it sweet.

But look around the room. At the next table a Japanese couple pour from a metal pot into hand-thrown cups without handles. Their menu is in Japanese, and chopsticks rest on their plates. The Tea Box, as chef Christine puts it, "is like New York: truly international."

Beautiful packaging with a natural look is a Takashimaya hallmark.

Sencha, a green tea, is Japan's favorite. It has a bright flavor with a gentle bitterness and a hint of sweetness.

Some Japanese metal teapots, like these, have interior sieves to hold the leaves.

Teatime at legendary Ladurée on the Champs-
Élysées indulges all the senses. A bedazzling choice
of pastries~including the most
famous cream-filled macaroons in
Paris~is dispensed here in an
atmosphere of sheer grandeur. If
you can tear yourself away from
the street-level bakery counter,
you'll be seated amid frescoes,
tasseled velvets, and gilded mirrors
in one of four upstairs tea salons
decorated in the opulent Second
Empire style. Though guests feel
swept back to an elegant past, this
shrine to posh and patisserie was
actually opened in 1997, a new

Ladurée's salons gleam with Napoleonic artifacts.

Luxurious time-out in Paris: 75, Avenue des Champs-Élysées

incarnation of Paris's first *salon de thé*, dating from the 1870s and still at 16, rue Royale. That was the era when Parisian women first sallied forth in public to meet friends, to see and be seen. Under ceilings where painted cherubs frolicked, gossip and flirtations flourished over the teacups.

All that awaits you at the new Ladurée, open for every meal from breakfast to after-opera snacks. But do visit for tea. The menu offers seventeen fine brews (the most popular a fragrant "blue tea" flavored with fruit), poured from silver teapots. The French don't take milk in their tea—perhaps all the better to balance the violet-flavored creams and the cloudlike charlottes on their dessert plates.

"The mere chink of cups and saucers turns the mind to happy repose." —George Gissie

Designed for a brief visit, but a glamorous one: the bar at Ladurée.

Long ago, a grandson of Ladurée's baker-founder had the idea of sandwiching two coconut macaroons together with a buttercream ganache. The invention became one of the quintessential tastes of Paris. Today

A Pastry Chef's Secrets of Sweet Success

What explains the superb quality of Ladurée's desserts? Says Philippe Andrieu, a fourth-generation pastry chef: "Careful consideration of flavor and texture, mouthwatering beauty, top-quality ingredients. And skill."

the Ladurée kitchens turn out some eight hundred large and three thousand mini-macaroons a day, in fifteen irresistible flavors, including chocolate, raspberry, lemon, rose petal, and ⌐a new addition by chef Philippe Andrieu⌐black currant with violet. "They must rest two days so the texture is perfect," he says, "light and crunchy outside, rich and melting inside. But the Ladurée recipe⌐that will always remain a secret."

A Glossary of Ladurée Goodness

Saint-Honoré
Light choux pastry, crunchy caramel, and rich cream.

Plaisirs Sucrés
Milk chocolate, hazelnuts, and praline.

Tentation
("Temptation!")
Dense chocolate cake layered with chocolate cream and strawberry jam.

Mille-Feuilles
Literally, "a thousand leaves." Light, caramelized pastry flavored with vanilla and rum, almonds and hazelnuts, lemon, or strawberries.

Tartes Of eight tartes offered, the favorite of ladies is strawberry-rhubarb.

Making Time
for Tea

Its heartening spirit will always soothe. From a light summer picnic to a fancy winter party, the restorative leaf can brighten your day.

I t needn't be an anniversary or a birthday for you and your beloved to indulge yourselves with a lavish breakfast in bed. What a cozy way to celebrate being together again after a business trip, or simply to say on any Sunday, "We're special, we deserve it." Turn off the phone, spread the newspaper all over the bed if you like, and read each other the best bits aloud. Make a pact: No weighty discussions about children or finances or car problems allowed.

Let the tray you present be just as special. Line it with one or two of your finest linen napkins ⁓ to soften the clinks and clangs ⁓ then "set the table" with the best silver pot and porcelain cups to fill with bracing Earl Grey or English breakfast tea. Add buttered crumpets and jam, perhaps several hard-boiled eggs, and this infrequent treat could easily become a new weekend ritual.

As your friend rushes down the hall to the meeting, she thinks no one at work knows it is her birthday. Suddenly the whole department begins singing to her. The tea tastes of roses, and the cookies are the prettiest she has ever seen.

Surprise celebrations are the merit raises we give each other. What could be more thoughtful—or easier—than cookies and tea? A simple teatime, for two or many, is a delightful, personal way to thank a friend for watching your child or trimming your hedge, to honor an accomplishment or get to know a new neighbor. Nothing fancy is required (unless it's the pastry), no great commitment of time is demanded—just a sense of surprise and gratitude to sweeten a single hour.

"Take some more tea," the March Hare said to Alice. "I've had nothing yet," Alice replied in an offended tone, "so I can't take more."

—Lewis Carroll, *Alice in Wonderland*

Bike it, hike it, or tuck it into the beach bag: Whatever repast one totes along always tastes better outdoors than in. But just as appetites sharpen in the open air, so does thirst. And nothing both quenches and invigorates like tea.

If it's just the two of you on an autumn day, carry along a thermos of tea and a pair of proper cups and saucers, carefully wrapped and protected in a pretty tea towel. Or, on a summer afternoon, pack a clear plastic jug and a few tea bags. With a source of clean water and a few leisurely hours, you can make sun tea (about eight tea bags to a quart), letting the heat of the sun unlock the brew's color and flavor. Prefer it chilled? Once the tea is "perked," nestle the jug between rocks in a cold mountain stream.

"One sip of this will bathe the drooping spirits in delight, beyond the bliss of dreams."

—John Milton

Early summer, filled with plighted troths and tossed bouquets, is a heavenly time for an afternoon garden party to celebrate a loving couple. Instead of cocktails, think of serving a tea-based punch, light enough to be enjoyed all afternoon. Add brewed tea to a blend of fresh lemon and orange juices, plus bottled cranberry juice, and pour over ice. Ginger ale (added at the last moment) gives it fizz. For something more sophisticated, try a golden tea "Bellini" punch: Fill the bowl with white wine and soda water (as if making a wine spritzer), add peach juice, tea, and some fresh strawberries.

"My experience... convinced me that tea was better than brandy."

—Theodore Roosevelt

A WELL-EARNED RESPITE

Many of us dream of working at home. Yet people who do often end up driving themselves the hardest. Their day whisks by without the quips and chats that co-workers can provide. The answer is a tea break. The custom started during England's industrial revolution, when workers were bent to their tasks as early as six in the morning. Though some employers attempted to do away with this "waste of time" in the mid-nineteenth century, such was the general outcry that the workers prevailed. So steep a small pot, retrieve a cup and saucer, and renew your spirit: The tea break has a long tradition.

"The spirit of the tea beverage is one of peace, comfort and refinement."

—Arthur Gray

One life is never enough. It's through our friends, above all, that we get to lead many lives, some close to ours, some branching far from our own experience. Perhaps that's why school and college reunions are often so exhilarating~like a mix of home movies and gripping novels.

A Reunion Tea: Books of Friendship

Friends Between Pages

"Julia,"
a chapter in
Pentimento
Lillian Hellman
As war clouds gather, a brave woman summons her childhood friend to risk a dangerous mission to Vienna.

Who Will Run the Frog Hospital?
Lorrie Moore
Teenage years are vividly recalled as two friends re-connect in Paris as adults.

Outer Banks
Anne Rivers Siddons
Former college chums resolve old jealousies and loyalties and stir up romance on a hurricane-swept seashore.

Talk Before Sleep
Elizabeth Berg
A tender, sad-funny story of women who gather to help a dying friend.

Connecting: The Enduring Power of Female Friendships
Sandy Sheehy
Nonfiction: A searching analysis through many lives and life stages.

But why wait for them? Plan your own reunion whenever a childhood friend is back in town, or write and invite your old college clique for an afternoon of sharing, hilarity, and tea. If everyone brings something good to eat, the effort is minimal. And the rewards? You'll recapture precious parts of your own life~ and be enriched by theirs.

TO SIP WITH SWEETS

Matching the flavors of teas to foods can be a great taste adventure, and not just for the connoisseur. Whether you're serving dessert after a meal or afternoon teatime sweets, consider trying these varieties.

With fruit-based desserts: Dragon Well, a Chinese green tea, or jasmine or Keemun, both oolongs.

With creamy or chocolate desserts: A hearty black tea, such as gold-tipped Assam from India or Earl Grey; Matcha, a bright Japanese green tea; or peppermint tea.

SPICY, SOUL-WARMING CHAI

Exotic, milky, and fragrant, chai is the ideal tea after a chilly autumn walk. The following is tea importer James Labe's quick, intensely flavorful recipe for a group: it makes twenty-four cups.

Add a quarter cup each of dried (not powdered) mace, ginger, cardamom, allspice, fennel seed, and coriander, plus two cloves, two star anise, and one cup of loose Assam tea leaves to one gallon cold water. Add three-quarters cup granulated sugar and a quarter teaspoon salt. Bring to a simmer on high heat; reduce heat to low. Add six cups whole milk and two cups half-and-half; simmer for a few minutes. Strain the chai, and serve.

In India, chai is everywhere—a folk tea, a comfort food.

AFTER THE WEDDING

A bride is the recipient of so much kindness that sometimes mere thank-you notes hardly seem adequate. For a heart overflowing with gratitude, an after-the-wedding tea is a meaningful way of showing appreciation to well-wishers of all generations. (Your parents' friends will be especially touched to be invited.) Serve a small copy of the wedding cake and romantic cookies that indicate "love is flourishing," and by all means use your guests' gifts, including every piece of that wedding-present china!

"In the South, you can't marry a man until you know how his Mama makes sweet tea."

—*Sweet Tea and Jesus Shoes*

It is a truth universally acknowledged that conversation flows happily over tea. Ah, yes...but which tea, exactly? If your book

For Your Book Club: Tea in a Literary Mode

"And suddenly the memory revealed itself. The taste was that of the little piece of madeleine which on Sunday morning at Cambray...my Aunt Leonie used to give me, dipping it first in her own cup of tea."
Swann's Way
Marcel Proust

club has planned to discuss an English novel of manners⁓the sort of gentle domestic drama that flows from Jane Austen to Barbara Pym⁓why not cue the tea to the genre, perhaps offering a delicate Darjeeling in porcelain cups with petite sandwiches of smoked salmon and curried egg salad? It's natural to pair books with sips and snacks. After all, so much literature is drenched in tea, from Henry James to Rosamunde Pilcher. Your book-mates will love the connection.

Whodunit?
Death on the Nile
Agatha Christie

The Daughter of Time
Josephine Tey

Serve English breakfast tea and fruit scones

Biography
Colette
Judith Thurman

Everyone Was So Young
Amanda Vaill

Serve oolong and madeleines

Classics
Madame Bovary
Gustave Flaubert

To the Lighthouse
Virginia Woolf

Serve Darjeeling and lemon cake

Distant Lands
The Poisonwood Bible
Barbara Kingsolver

Corelli's Mandolin
Louis de Bernières

Serve orange pekoe and pita with eggplant puree

Women's Lives
Tell Me a Riddle
Tillie Olsen

Final Payments
Mary Gordon

Serve chamomile and fruit tartlets

Tea is a great settler of the soul—and often of the digestive system. Perhaps that's why in Jane Austen's day it was taken not at four in the afternoon but after dinner. There by the parlor fire, as the family read or played a game of whist, sweets and tea helped while away the evening.

Herbal teas (properly called tisanes) are ideal for evening, since they are not derived from the tea plant but, rather, from the herbs and so contain no caffeine. To ease digestion, try ginger tea or linden. Peppermint tea (or a peppermint-spearmint blend) has a similar reputation. But to shed the tensions of the day, nothing soothes like chamomile. Tisanes are best appreciated without milk.

"Enjoy life sip by sip, not gulp by gulp."

—The Minister of Leaves

WOULD YOU CARE TO DANCE?

Where, in the 1880s, could a young lady and her beau disport themselves properly? Why, at a tea dance, held at the tea court of a fine hotel, complete with potted palms and sedate violins. Like the fashionable tea gardens of a century earlier, which drew hundreds for dancing, strolling, and refreshments, tea dances in England and America were not just upper-crust affairs. For city working girls, far from home and family, they offered a sanctioned way to socialize. And by the time the dance craze of the 1920s hit, so many girls were kicking up their heels at teatime that even fashion followed—with short and shimmery dresses that freed the legs at last.

Isn't it time to revive the custom? For a social club, fund-raiser, or holiday afternoon, a tea dance

(teenagers welcome) can be a delightful event. Who can resist the chance to wear a swirly skirt, nibble pretty cakes, and dance to live musicians who remember the waltz and the fox trot? Even grandparents might be tempted to twirl across the dance floor⁓or at least tap a toe at tables around the perimeter. Held at the propitious hours of 4 to 6:30 in the afternoon, a tea dance wakes up the senses with some genteel fun.

"At an afternoon tea, the debutante wears an evening dress⁓a very simple evening dress, but an evening dress all the same."

—Emily Post

As night falls, we too often review unfinished tasks and predict future ones~not exactly a recipe for slumber. But sleep is precious: It not only "knits up the ravelled sleeve of care," as Shakespeare wrote; it also restores the body's defenses. Time-honored inducements to sleep include a hot bath, warm milk, some Mozart~and a relaxing cup of chamomile. Sweet thoughts help, too. Evoke them by brewing a particularly fragrant herbal blend~ perhaps one with roses, hibiscus, lemongrass, or black currant leaf. The floral notes have an uplifting effect, helping you recall the day's perfect moments: a glimpse of children leaping puddles, a letter from a friend, the flame-colored maple trees at sunset. Let these happy memories bear you to sleep, glad, as one Sidney Smith put it, "I was not born before tea."

"Now stir the fire and close the shutters fast. And while the bubbling and loud hissing urn throws up a steamy column...let us welcome peaceful ev'ning in."

—William Cowper

Resources

The British Shoppe and Gourmet Merchants
45 Wall Street
Madison, CT 06443
(800) 842-6674
www.thebritishshoppe.com
Traditional British teas, foods, cheeses, and tea accessories. The Front Parlour Tearoom offers lunch and afternoon tea.

Chewton Glen
New Milton, Hampshire
BH25 6QS, England
(800) 344-5087
www.chewtonglen.com
A country manor-house hotel offering traditional afternoon tea.

The Cultured Cup
5346 Belt Line Road
Dallas, TX 75240
(888) 847-8327
www.theculturedcup.com
A variety of teas, including Mariage Frères from France, as well as tea accessories and foods.

Dabney Herbs
P.O. Box 22061
Louisville, KY 40252
(502) 893-5198
www.dabneyherbs.com
A wide variety of organically grown herbal teas.

Eastern Shore Tea Company
9 West Aylesbury Road
Lutherville, MD 21093
(800) 823-1408
www.baltlcoffee.com
A variety of loose teas and tea bags in decorativee bags and tins.

Lalith Guy Paranavitana Empire Tea Services
5155 Hartford Avenue
Columbus, IN 47203
(812) 375-1937
www.empiretea.com
Fine whole leaf teas, tea foods, tea accessories, and books.

Grace Tea Company, Ltd.
50 West 17th Street
New York, NY 10011
(212) 255-2935
www.gracetea.com
Rare teas from China, Formosa (Taiwan), India, and Ceylon (Sri Lanka) that are packageds in elegant black metal canisters.

Harney & Sons Fine Teas
P.O. Box 665
Salisbury, CT 06068
(800) TEATIME
www.harney.com
A wide variety of teas, tea accessories, tea foods, and gifts.

In Pursuit of Tea
P. O. Box 1284
Cooper Station
New York, NY 10003
(866) TRUETEA;
718-302-0780
www.truetea.com
Over 30 types of teas from remote regions of the world, including white, green, black, and oolong teas, as well as tea accessories.

Ladurée
75, Avenue des Champs-Élysées
75008 Paris
France
01 45 63 45 79
www.laduree.fr
Founded in 1862, this famous tea salon and patisserie offers a small selection of carefully chosen fine teas.

Lisa's Tea Treasures
1875 South Bascom Avenue
Suite 165
Campbell, CA 95008
(408) 371-7377
www.lisasteatreasurescampbell.surf
metro.com
A wide variety of teas, including black, flavored black, tisanes, and their own special tea blend, as well as tea accessories, gift sets, and a Victorian-style tearoom.

The Little Teapot
9401 Montpelier Drive
Laurel, MD 20708
(301) 498-8486
www.the-little-teapot.com
Teas, British foods, accessories, fine china, and tea books. Tea is served in the Montpelier Mansion twice monthly.

Republic of Tea
8 Digital Drive, Suite 100
Novato, CA 94949
(800) 711-8768
www.republicoftea.com
A wide variety of teas, display tins, tea pots, and other tea accessories.

Rose Tree Cottage
828 E. California Boulevard
Pasadena, CA 91108
626-793-3337
www.rosetreecottage.com
A traditional English Tea Room and shop, serving English Afternoon Tea. An extensive variety of fine British teas and foods are available to order.

San Francisco Herb Company
250 14th Street
San Francisco, CA 94103
(800) 227-4530
www.sfherb.com
A variety of loose bulk herbal teas, as well as some other teas.

Simpson & Vail
3 Quarry Road
Brookfield, CT 06804
(800) 282-8327;
(203) 775-0240
www.svtea.com
Over 150 tea varieties, as well as tea foods and tea accessories.

SpecialTeas
2 Reynolds Street
Norwalk, CT 06855
(888) ENJOY-TEA
www.specialteas.com
Over 300 varieties of loose-leaf teas and tea blends, as well as tea accessories.

The Tea Box at Takashimaya
693 Fifth Avenue
New York, NY 10022
(800) 753-2038
A tea salon offering a wide variety of loose teas, including green tea, black tea, flavored black tea, and herbal tea blends sold by the ounce.

Tealuxe
0 Brattle Street
Cambridge, MA 02138
(888) TEALUXE
www.tealuxe.com
Over 100 varieties of teas, sold by the gram, as well as gift sets and other tea accessories.

Tea-n-Crumpets
1105 E. Francisco Boulevard, #4
San Rafael, CA 94901
(415) 457-2495
www.tea-n-crumpets.com
A wide variety of teas from around the world. Also offers crumpets, preserves, and tea accessories.

Todd & Holland Tea Merchants
7577 Lake Street
River Forest, IL 60305
(800) 747-8327
www.todd-holland.com
Over 200 varieties of loose-leaf teas, as well as tea samplers, tea tours, and an extensive collection of tea pots, tea accessories, and books.

Upton Tea Imports
34 Hayden Rowe Street
Hopkinton, MA 01748
(800) 234-8327
www.uptontea.com
Over 300 varieties of loose-leaf teas, as well as tea accessories.

Mark T. Wendell Tea Company
50 Beharrell Street
West Concord, MA 01742
(978) 369-3709
www.marktwendell.com
A large selection of fine teas and accessories, imported from around the world. Offered in both loose bulk containers and tea bags.

Contact the above sources individually for information about hours and ordering by telephone, fax, e-mail, Web sites, or mail order.

Photography Credits

Index